HOPE & HEALING SERIES

WHEN YOUR CHILD DIES

THERESA M. HUNTLEY

I0647491

Augsburg
MINNEAPOLIS

*Dedicated to my family: my husband—Mike—
with whom I have shared both deep loss and great joy,
and to my children—Molly, Megan, John, Kaitlyn, and
Jimmy—who are daily reminders of the precious gift of life.*

Other books in the Hope and Healing series:
When Your Child Loses a Loved One
When Your Parent Dies
When Your Friend Dies
When Your Spouse Dies
When Your Baby Dies through Miscarriage or Stillbirth

Large-quantity purchases or custom editions of this book are available at a discount from the pub-
lisher. For more information, contact the sales department at Augsburg Fortress, Publishers, 1-800-
328-4648, or write to: Sales Director, Augsburg Fortress, Publishers, P.O. Box 1209, Minneapolis, MN
55440-1209.

Scripture passages are from the New Revised Standard Version of the Bible, copyright © 1946, 1952,
1971, 1989 by the Division of Christian Education of the National Council of the Churches of Christ in
the USA. Used by permission.

Cover design by David Meyer; cover image from PhotoDisc, Inc.
Book design by Michelle L. N. Cook

Library of Congress Cataloging-in-Publication Data
Huntley, Theresa, 1961-
   When your child dies / Theresa M. Huntley.
   p.cm.
   Includes bibliographical references.
   ISBN 0-8066-4261-0
   1. Bereavement—Psychological aspects. 2. Death—Psychological aspects. 3. Grief. 4. Children—
Death. I. Title.
BF575.G7.H87 2001
155.9'37—dc21   2001027947

The paper used in this publication meets the minimum requirements of American National
Standard for Information Sciences—Permanence of Paper for Printed Library Materials, ANSI
Z329.48-1984.

Manufactured in the U.S.A.

CONTENTS

INTRODUCTION

Your child has died, and you are now faced with what likely seems inconceivable—life without your child. You have been forced to embark on a journey that is vastly different than any you have taken before. Nothing could have prepared you for this loss or for the intensity of the grief that accompanies it. The death of a child is like no other. Your life has been irrevocably changed; you will never again be the person you were before the your child's death. Life is different. You are different. Your days stretch before you endlessly, filled with a pain that is deeper than any you have ever before felt. Your life has been shattered; your heart has been pierced. A part of you has died. Will you always feel the overwhelming emptiness? Will you ever again experience a sense of wholeness?

Does life have meaning if your child is no longer here to share it with you?

Let me begin by saying that I am very sorry for your loss. Although I do not know you or your child, I am sensitive to the pain you are experiencing. While I cannot change the reality that your child has died, I do want to provide you with some information to guide you on your grief journey. In doing this, I hope to offer a sense that life can again be full and meaningful.

As much as your life feels as if it has come to a screeching halt, you may have noticed that the world around you has not ceased to function. Life goes on, whether we are prepared for this or not. As difficult as it may seem—in the face of your loss and the overwhelming turmoil it has created—at some point down the road you will come to the realization that you have a choice to make. Although you cannot alter the fact that your child has died, you can make a decision as to how you will live your life without him or her. You can face your grief and begin a journey upon which you will integrate the death of your son or daughter into the fabric of your life. Or you can avoid the pain and attempt to bury it deep within.

The simple fact that you are reading this book seems to indicate that you are choosing the former. Although the road may be long and winding, it is my hope that you will learn to live with your loss and to embrace the meaning it will ultimately have in your life.

❧

As you begin this journey it will be important for you to take special care of yourself. Death exacts a heavy price, and grief demands a tremendous effort—physically, mentally, emotionally, and spiritually.

Grief can be overwhelming, filling you with emotions that threaten to consume you. Although your grief will be yours and yours alone, know that you do not have to traverse the road alone. There are others who are willing to walk beside you on this journey, others who want to help you carry the burden of your grief. To ask for their help—and then to accept their assistance—are gifts that can help to heal your wounded heart.

As you face the intense grief you are now experiencing, consider how you have coped with difficult experiences in the past. Which were helpful coping strategies for you, and which were not? In times of crisis, people tend to rely on that which is familiar and comfortable, regardless of whether or not it is beneficial to them. Realize that now is probably not the time to expect yourself to successfully take on new behaviors or coping strategies. Try to draw upon your previous strengths as best you can, taking care to be gentle with yourself.

❧

My purpose in writing this book is to offer guidance as you grieve the death of your child. The book can be read from beginning to end or you can choose those sections that are most useful to you at a particular time. It will offer you general information about grief, describing the experience and offering varying ways of understanding it. I will talk about the different ways that men, women and children grieve, and discuss how your child's death affects the various relationships in your life.

For ease in reading, I have chosen to use the female gender when the assumption of male or female is ambiguous. In doing this there is no intention on my part to suggest that one gender is more or less important than the other.

Be gentle with yourself as you begin this grief journey.

CHAPTER 1

DEFINING GRIEF WHEN YOUR CHILD DIES

The death of your child may have been something you've been anticipating in light of a serious illness or it may have come as a complete surprise in the form of an accident, a suicide, or a murder. Whatever the case, your life has been irrevocably changed. Your child has died, and you will never again be the same.

The death of a child has frequently been described as the worst loss. The grief that ensues is deep—and potentially disabling—and is said to endure longer than any other. Your life has been devastated. The child you have loved and cared for has died. He or she will never again be physically present in your life.

A future without your son or daughter is not something you probably ever considered. The death of a child goes against the natural order of life; it has robbed or cheated you of the hopes and dreams you had for your child. As a parent, you may feel that you have failed your child because somehow you were unable to protect her from death. The pain is unbearable; it may be unrelenting. Some moments or events of each day you will recall vividly; others will seem like a blur. This may go on for a long time. It is likely difficult to imagine how you will get through each hour of each day and yet—somehow—the days do pass by. Time moves forward, and life, whether you are prepared for it or not, does go on. When you are ready, you will, too.

DEFINING GRIEF AND MOURNING

Initially when your child dies you will be consumed by your grief with every waking moment of every day seeming somehow to hold a reminder of your child or your child's death. Parents, when speaking of this, frequently state that it is often only upon awakening that they have a brief period when they have completely forgotten that their child has died. Quickly enough, however, remembrance comes and the grief washes over them again. Making the choice to get up each day requires a determined effort. Facing what the day holds (be it managing a household, caring for other children, or a job) presents an additional hurdle. For a while you may need help to assist with household responsibilities or provide care for other children if you have them. If you're employed outside the home, you may need some time off to be with your family before returning to work on a regular basis.

At some point, however, it will be necessary for you to pick up the pieces of your life and to re-establish a routine for yourself. You will be faced with the challenge of constructing a life in which your child is no longer physically present, but their memory is carried within your heart. The intense pain that has been your primary connection to your deceased child will be replaced by an emotional connection that enables you to remember and honor your child, while at the same time allowing you to live a life that once again contains meaning and hope. Achieving this point will be the hard and painful work of grief.

Grief is a process that can be defined as a normal, internalized reaction to a loss. Mourning is a part of grief and involves a person's adaptation to the loss.

Grieving is undoubtedly the most painful work we are called upon to do and yet, at the same time, it is absolutely essential that we do it. Grief is not something that will simply go away with the passage of time or a determined effort to ignore or avoid it. When someone we love dies, it is as if our lives stop. We become immobilized by our loss. If we don't grieve—for whatever reason—our lives remain stuck. The work of grief—of coming to terms with the reality that our loved one has died—is ultimately what enables us to move ahead with our life, however altered it might now be.

When talking about grieving, Barbara D. Rosof, in her book *The Worst Loss,* states that it is only by allowing yourself to grieve that you can move toward a time and a place where the pain does not consume you. "This is a paradox: Only by allowing yourself to feel the most intense and shattering pain can you move toward a life in which pain is not the center. It is paradoxical, yet it is simply how human beings are built" (p. 51).

As you begin this grief journey it may be helpful to have a general sense of what lies ahead. Although your grief is unique, there will be some aspects of it that you share with all bereaved parents. Typically there will be a period of acute grief, which is then followed by the much longer process of mourning. Initially it may feel as if you are flooded with your grief. This may seem to go on for a long time, often as long as four to six months. Gradually, however, it will begin to ebb and flow, providing you with brief periods of respite in the midst of the intensity. In *The Bereaved Parent,* Harriet Sarnoff Schiff speaks to the helpfulness of knowing that others before you have shared your pain when she states:

> "We bereaved parents come in all ages. We are not limited to any specific color or faith. Parents with dead babies, parents whose sons died in war, parents who are elderly and lived to bury their middle-aged children, all have a great need to know that others have experienced the emotions they are feeling and

that these others are dealing effectively with both their bereavement and life" (p. xiii–xiv).

It may also be beneficial to have an idea of a time-frame for how long your grief will last. As I say this, it is critical to note that grief is not something that you will "get over" as many people frequently think (i.e., "Haven't you gotten over it yet? It's been six months" or "I thought you would have been over that by now. What's wrong with you?"). There is a general consensus that, when a child dies, the timetable for grief has to be expanded. Parents are encouraged to allow themselves a minimum of one to two years to get to the point where their grief isn't at the center of their awareness. It may then take an additional one to two years for parents to feel as if they have regained some semblance of their life as it was prior to their child's death. Many bereaved parents note a change in their grief at about four to six months following the death. They sense a lessening of the intensity of it and begin to have a renewed aware-ness of life.

Rosof notes that a number of bereaved parents cite periods in the second or third year after their child died as being even more painful than the first year. It was during these times when parents emerged into the pro-found realization that their son or daughter was dead and would never be coming back. As difficult as this deeper realization is to experience, however, you will—in a way—be in a better position to engage with it. You have lived with your grief and survived what you once believed to be unbearable.

Whether you can admit it or not, there is some degree of comfort to be gained from this awareness. Although your life will never again be the same, you realize that within you lies the strength to face the challenge of rebuilding your life without your child physically present in it. You cannot change the fact that your child has died. You can, however, decide how you will live a life that not only honors the memory of your child, but one that again holds meaning and purpose.

Your timetable for grief will be your own. How long it lasts will be influenced by a number of factors that can include: 1) the circumstances of the death, 2) the nature of the relationship you had with your child, 3) your previous experience with death or other difficult experiences, 4) your ability to cope, 5) the strength of your support network, and 6) your current life circumstances.

CHAPTER 2

UNDERSTANDING GRIEF AND THE TASKS OF MOURNING

Grief is an ongoing process. People respond to any loss over time. The meaning that the loss has for people may change as one's understanding and perspective of what has been lost is periodically evaluated and re-evaluated. Although your grief will become less intense, it won't ever completely go away; it is something that will remain forever as a part of the fabric of your life. Just as the deceased was a part of your life, so too will be your memories of her and the meaning that her death holds for you.

A number of grief educators have proposed that grief be viewed as having stages or phases. Others have associated tasks with grief, suggesting that these tasks not only comprise the work of grief, but also offer a means for understanding it.

Many people are familiar with the pioneering work of Dr. Elizabeth Kubler-Ross. Through her work with people who were dying, Kubler-Ross recognized that there appeared to be stages that were experienced by these patients. The stages she identified are: denial, anger, bargaining, depression, and acceptance. People responded to these stages quite literally and it was assumed, therefore, that people who were dying would pass through them sequentially in an orderly fashion.

This general misinterpretation of Kubler-Ross's work when it is applied to grief is unfortunate in that it conflicts with the current perspective of grief as an ongoing process. It does not allow for the idea that people move through the proposed stages in varying order or that they may experience them more than once or not at all. It is my impression that Kubler-Ross understood that dying and grief are processes and that they should not be viewed as rigid or linear.

The phases of grief that you may hear people reference include the following: 1) shock and disbelief, 2) searching and yearning, 3) disorganization and despair, and 4) rebuilding and healing. Just in the naming of these, you may have a sense of what is involved in each. Initially upon learning of a death a person experiences a period of numbness. This numbness enables a person to disregard the fact of the loss for a brief period of time; it provides, in a way, a break from something that seems unbearable. The next phase, yearning, involves a searching both for the deceased and for the meaning of their death, as well as a yearning for the return of the person who has died. In the third phase, the phase of disorganization and despair, the grieving person experiences difficulty functioning in the environment. The fourth phase, rebuilding and healing, finds the person gradually beginning to pull the pieces of their life back into some type of order.

What is important to note with both stages and phases is that movement through them does not occur in a neat and orderly manner. There may be overlaps, and people may find themselves working and reworking their way through the various stages and phases. At times this can be very confusing, and parents may find themselves wondering if perhaps they are going "crazy." Rest assured that you are not; it's all part of the process.

In considering the experience of grief, I have found William Worden's four tasks of mourning helpful. Not only do these tasks define the "grief work" that he believes must be completed for healing to occur, they also provide a means for understanding grief. Worden states that although the tasks are not specifically ordered, there is some ordering suggested in their definitions.

Task I: To Accept the Reality of the Loss

Whenever a person dies—even in the event of an anticipated death—there is always an element of disbelief. When a child dies, parents may think such things as, "This can't be happening; it's like a really bad dream" or "They must be talking about someone else. They can't be talking about my child." The first task of mourning involves facing the reality that the person is dead; that they are gone and will never again return to be a part of your daily life.

Searching and yearning are directly related to the accomplishment of this task. You may find yourself calling out to your child or you may catch a glimpse of another child, mistakenly identifying them as your son or daughter, having then to remind yourself, "No, that isn't my child. My child died." In doing this, you are gradually moving toward an acceptance of the fact that your child is no longer alive.

The opposite of accepting the reality of the loss is not believing through some type of denial. Although denial does serve the purpose of protecting you briefly from the painful reality of your child's death, if maintained over a long period of time it can interfere with your acceptance of the situation and your healing. One example of denial is the parent who leaves their child's room exactly as it was prior to their child's death for many years, keeping it in a shrine-like state. Another is the parent who does the opposite, quickly removing everything that reminds them of their deceased child. Most parents seem to find a balance. When ready, they sort through their child's things, carefully selecting those items that will provide comfort in the years to come.

It is important to note that coming to an acceptance of the reality of the loss takes time. This, states

Worden, is because working through denial involves not only an intellectual acceptance, but an emotional one as well. Although you may be cognitively aware of the finality of your child's death, it may take longer for your emotions to allow full acceptance of it. Participation in traditional rituals such as the funeral can be helpful in assisting you in moving toward acceptance.

TASK II: TO WORK THROUGH TO THE PAIN OF GRIEF

The process of grieving involves acknowledging and working through the various feelings that are a part of mourning. Although people grieve in similar and predictable ways, it is imperative that we recognize the uniqueness of the experience for each individual. Just as the relationship between you and your child was unique, so too will be your sense of loss.

Whenever someone we love—or have a significant relationship with—dies, we will experience pain. Although the intensity and expression may vary, the fact of its presence does not. It is, therefore, absolutely essential to face the pain and experience it fully in order to grieve effectively. If a person avoids or suppresses it, this will serve only to prolong their grief process. The intense pain will not simply go away; it will remain buried deep within you until it can be addressed properly at a later time.

It is unfortunate that oftentimes our society—rather than supporting the mourner's need to grieve—actually discourages people from working through their pain. Whether they are intentionally conveyed or not, messages are given which indicate that it is not okay grieve.

The opposite of working through the pain is not to feel. People can attempt to avoid their painful feelings by doing such things as: avoiding people and things that remind them of their loved one, remembering only the positive qualities of the deceased, consuming alcohol or drugs, over focusing on a hobby, or working to the point of exhaustion each day. Although these activities enable you to avoid facing your feelings for a time, in the end they cannot replace the work of grieving.

Task III: To Adjust to an Environment in Which the Deceased Is Missing

Worden states that adjusting to a new environment means different things to different people, depending on what the relationship was with the dead person and the various roles the deceased played. It is not unusual for it to take some time after the loss for the bereaved person to realize fully what it is like to live without the person who has died.

The bereaved person may be faced with: 1) adjusting to the loss of the roles previously played by the deceased, 2) adjusting to their own sense of self, and 3) adjusting to one's sense of the world. It will be necessary for them to learn new roles, develop new skills, and face life with a new understanding or perspective of it.

As a parent you may feel as if you have no one to take care of now that your child has died. Your roles as caregiver and protector have been stripped from you. Your personal faith may be seriously challenged, and you may question the fairness and meaning of a life in which children die.

The opposite of adjusting is to not adapt to the loss. Although there may be a temptation to permanently withdraw from the world—thus avoiding the necessary adaptations—most people do not take this course. They choose, instead, to live their life without the deceased, ultimately integrating the implications of the death into their daily lives.

Task IV: To Emotionally Relocate the Deceased and Move on with Life

When a person dies, Worden states that people are faced with the task of finding an appropriate place for the dead in their emotional lives—one that will enable them to go on living effectively in the world. For bereaved parents, the thought of emotional withdrawal may feel particularly threatening; it's as if in withdrawing, they fear the loss of their child on an even deeper level.

The task, however, is not to give up the relationship with your child, but rather to develop a new connection with her. The thoughts and memories that you associate with your deceased child will never be lost; they will always be a part of you. They must over time, however, be relocated in your emotional life if you are to move forward with life. When people hold on to a past attachment or relationship, it can prevent them from being able to go on and develop new ones. The fact that they move on and establish new relationships does not in any way minimize the love they had for the deceased. It signals, rather, that there are other people to love and they are ready to begin to live life again.

CHAPTER 3

THE AFFECTS OF GRIEF

Grief is a process. It is experienced over time and becomes a part of one's life history. Grief can affect you physically, mentally, emotionally, and spiritually. It is not uncommon to hear bereaved people say they feel as if they are going crazy. Having an awareness of the multiple affects of grief normalizes your experience and makes it feel less isolating.

Although your grieving will be a unique experience, you'll likely note that many of the reactions described in this section will be exhibited by you at some point on your grief journey. Some will be manifested soon after the death, whereas others may be delayed.

PHYSICAL AFFECTS

The physical affects associated with grief include the following: fatigue/lack of energy, shortness of breath, dry mouth, tightness in the chest, tightness in the throat, hollowness in the stomach, weakness in the muscles, increased illness, and a sense of depersonalization, feeling as if nothing seems real, including yourself. These sensations, when noted, can be rather frightening.

If you experience the physical symptoms for a long time or are worried about them, contact your primary physician and set up an appointment. More often than not, a physical exam will reveal that there is nothing seriously wrong with you. Consulting with your physician will give you an opportunity to verbalize your concerns, as well as provide reasonable reassurance that bodily distress is a part of the grieving process and will eventually abate.

MENTAL AFFECTS

There are a number of thought patterns associated with the grief experience. Some occur in the initial period of grief and disappear fairly soon, whereas others persist for longer periods and can sometimes trigger feelings that can lead to depression or anxiety. The thought patterns grieving parents most often describe include: disbelief, confusion, lack of concentration, difficulty making decisions, preoccupation, and a sense of the child's presence.

Upon learning of your child's death you initially may have experienced an overwhelming sense of disbelief. Parents frequently comment that it feels as if they are in a bad dream. This is particularly true if the death was sudden.

You may experience difficulty paying attention for any length of time. Allow yourself room for mistakes, realizing you are not thinking as clearly as you typically would.

You may also find yourself thinking constantly about your deceased child. There seem to be reminders wherever you look, and you may worry that they will always cause you pain. In an attempt to find some relief, you may want to withdraw from the people, activities, and things that remind you of your child. Although this may seem tempting, avoidance will not make the pain go away. As a part of your healing it will be helpful to share your memories and talk about your feelings with others.

In the time shortly following the death, you may sense your child's presence, thinking that you see, hear, or feel her. Bereaved parents typically find this helpful.

EMOTIONAL AFFECTS

The emotional experience of grief can be quite intense. Gradually as you allow yourself to experience the feelings, their intensity will lessen. The emotions commonly associated with grief include: sadness, anger, guilt, helplessness, anxiety, loneliness, shock, numbness, yearning, rage, and intense feelings.

Sadness is the feeling most commonly experienced by the bereaved. Often—but not always—it is accompanied by crying. Some parents report feeling as if they cried all of the time; others stated they struggled fiercely to avoid tears, fearing that if they started crying they would not be able to stop. Everyone is different when it comes to this. Do what feels comfortable realizing, however, that avoiding your sadness will not make it go away.

Anger is also frequently experienced as a part of grieving. This can stem from a feeling of helplessness or a loss of control. Typically, anger will be directed outwardly at God, another person, or perhaps even your child who has died. Occasionally, however, it will be directed inward and experienced as guilt or self-reproach. This is especially true for bereaved parents. As a part of your healing, it will be important for you to find ways to express your anger rather than letting it fester inside.

Shock is defined by Barbara Rosof as a physical and psychological emergency reaction, a way of slowing everything down, of warding off facts too horrible, too overwhelming to take in. It is an involuntary response that you have no ability to control. Shock occurs most often in the case of a sudden death, but it can also be present in the case of a lingering illness where the death is somewhat anticipated.

SPIRITUAL AFFECTS

When considering how grief affects you spiritually, it is important to draw a distinction between religion and spirituality. Religion can be defined as the organized or formal expression of one's beliefs that is shared in a faith community. Spirituality is comprised of your deepest personal convictions. It serves to provide meaning and purpose for your life and can connect you with a faith system or higher power of some kind.

When people experience the death of a significant person in their life, it is not uncommon for them to find themselves in a period of profound questioning—a time in which they may struggle deeply with previously held beliefs. As parents, you have been confronted with the painful reality that you cannot always protect your children; death can happen in spite of your best intentions and the love and attention you have freely given. You may be left questioning the senselessness of your child's death, wondering what was the meaning in her pain and suffering. You realize that bad things can in fact happen and that life is not always fair. What you once thought was important prior to your child's death, may now seem irrelevant or pointless in the face of what has happened; it may feel as if your life has no direction or purpose.

Ideally you will be able to define or create some meaning for your child's death and to live with the changes that were imposed as a part of the loss. Ultimately you will come to let go of life as you have known it and move forward with the memory and spirit of your child carried within your heart. You will remember and honor your child, while at the same time living a life that once again holds meaning and hope. In this process your spirituality—your original life values and philosophical beliefs—will either be affirmed and strengthened or adjusted in some way.

Chapter 4

MEN'S, WOMEN'S, AND CHILDREN'S GRIEF

The death of your child affects not only you, but the people you are in relationship with as well. It is helpful to realize that although you and the other people are all grieving the loss of the same person—your child—your grief experiences will be unique. Not only is your connection to the deceased different—be it as a mother or father, sister or brother, grandmother or grandfather, aunt or uncle, neighbor or friend—your relationship with the child was different as well. Your child was special to each of you; you must all grieve what you have lost in your own way and in your own time.

The way in which each of you deals with your grief will be influenced by a number of factors that can include gender, family of origin, history of previous losses, and current life circumstances. Although you may not agree with how someone is handling their grief, having an awareness of what might be influencing their response will hopefully enable you to be somewhat more tolerant regarding your differences.

In this chapter, I will discuss the ways in which men, women, and children grieve differently.

MEN'S GRIEF

The following description is a generalization; although it may apply to most men, it won't fit for all.

Men are accustomed to focusing on the task at hand and getting the job done; they are much less inclined to consider the emotional aspects—the feelings and relationships—of a situation. If the goal is to complete the task, then attending to your feelings—or to the feelings of others—will naturally be viewed as secondary.

Men have tended to be taught to suppress their feelings, rather than learning ways of expressing them. For boys who grew up in an environment that conveyed the message "big boys don't cry"—one in which feelings were considered to be a sign of weakness—there was limited opportunity for self-awareness regarding not only what they were feeling, but also how to express those feelings.

For many fathers, the deepest pain comes from their perceived inability to protect their child from death. Although we know on a rational level that we do not have complete control over all that happens in life, men in particular seem to be conditioned to thinking that providing for their family and keeping them safe is their first priority.

Without intending it, fathers may be given the message that it is not okay to ask for support for themselves. Some dads speak of feeling as if they "had to be strong" for their family; as if they had to take care of the needs of their family, which may have meant neglecting or avoiding their own.

Men may also have the idea that it is their responsibility to move forward with life, to get on with the process of living. Facing one's feelings of grief—as overwhelming and disabling as that can be at times—can be seen as conflicting with this. Fathers who have faced their pain and learned ways to express their feelings have, however, found the opposite to be true. Doing the difficult work of grief has enabled them to integrate the death and begin the process of reconstructing their lives.

WOMEN'S GRIEF

As noted above, the following description is a generalization; although it may apply to most women, it won't fit for all.

Most women are accustomed to focusing on the emotional aspects of a situation. They have typically been raised with the understanding that relationships provide the framework for their lives, and the maintenance of these relationships is something to which women are committed. As a part of this commitment, it is necessary for women to be attuned to their own feelings, as well as to those of the people around them.

In general, women talk about their feelings much more than men do and they have a greater sense of comfort in doing this. As Barbara D. Rosof states in *The Worst Loss,* "For many more women than men, revealing that they feel scared or sad or inadequate is a statement of fact; it is not an admission of failure. Asking for support is a practical response, not a defeat" (p. 95).

Some mothers talk of their intense need to express their feelings and to talk of their deceased child. When their partners have difficulty engaging with this need, women frequently feel isolated in their grief. At times they may even question whether or not the father is experiencing grief, rather than considering that they are coping in the way they know how or in the way they think is expected of them.

CHILDREN'S GRIEF

If you have other children, it will be beneficial to have knowledge about how their grieving process differs from yours as an adult. It is important to note that differences do exist, and that the younger the age of the child the more pronounced these differences will be. Rosof suggests five principle ways in which children's grief differs from that of adults. She states that children: 1) are more physical, 2) are less verbal, 3) express their anger very directly, 4) need respites, and 5) attune themselves to parents' needs.

Children have a tendency to experience and express intense emotions in physical ways. Engaging aggressively in physical activity can provide them with an outlet for the expression of these feelings. Children may also express their grief through physical symptoms, some of which may be similar to those of the deceased prior to the death.

Even children who are verbally quite competent are likely to experience some degree of difficulty articulating the intense feelings that are a part of their grief process. Your child will look to you for help in finding the words that go with the emotions they are having.

Children will also cope with their feelings through play activities. These activities provide children with a means of expression, as well as allowing them to become more comfortable with what likely had been unfamiliar to them.

Children have a tendency to act out their anger and you may notice your child being more physically aggressive with others. They may also engage in increased verbal fighting or just seem mad for no apparent reason. Obviously it will be important to acknowledge their feeling, while also guiding them to appropriate expressions for their anger.

It is difficult to deal with the intensity of grief for long periods of time. Children—both because of their limited tolerance for emotional pain and their still developing coping skills—have a particular need to take breaks from the often overwhelming and consuming aspects of the grieving process. The fact that your child grieves in spurts—at times obviously very aware of their sibling's death and the implications for their life and others seemingly oblivious to this—does not mean that she is not grieving.

Children—more often than we realize and certainly more extensively than we give them credit for—are aware of and accommodating to the emotional atmosphere in their home. When your child observes you in the depths of your own grief, they may make a judgment as to how much of their feelings you will be able to handle. If they sense—be it accurate or not—that you are unable to handle their emotions, they will attempt to protect you by limiting the feelings they share with you. It will be important to periodically touch base with your child regarding how she is doing. This will minimize the chance that your child will hide her grief from you for long periods because she has the erroneous impression that you cannot bear it.

CHAPTER 5

GRIEF AND YOUR RELATIONSHIPS

When your child dies, it may feel as if your life has ended and the world has stopped. Although the physical relationship with your child has ended, your relationships with other people in your life have not. Somehow—as you struggle to work through your grief each day—you have to figure out how to relate to the people around you.

How these people—your family and friends, colleagues and neighbors—respond to your grief will vary. At a time when you are most vulnerable, you will likely find that you have the task of educating other people about your loss and the needs you have related to it. Given how overwhelming this may seem, it might be beneficial to consider the affect of your loss on the following relationships.

Although you may not be able to change how people respond to your grief, the information may be helpful to you in managing your ongoing relationships.

Hopefully it can assist you in deciding whether or not to engage with those people who are genuinely trying to offer support—as uncomfortable or awkward as this can be at times—as well enabling you to be somewhat more tolerant of those who may have unrealistic expectations of you. Some people—as they learn more about your loss and the journey you are on—will be able to accommodate your needs. Others may be unwilling or unable to do this for any number of reasons.

RELATIONSHIP WITH YOUR PARTNER

When your child dies, you and your partner both grieve. The child who has died may have been the biological or adopted child of both of you or she may have become a part of your family through a committed relationship (i.e., a partnership or marriage). Whatever the case, you are both affected. Given your shared loss, your ability to be available and responsive to one another's needs is seriously compromised.

Openness to your differences in grieving is critical. Part of this will evolve from the realization that you cannot be totally dependent upon the relationship with your partner in this process; you gradually learn to accept one another as separate people, with individual needs and different ways of dealing with them. It will be essential for you to maintain awareness of your partner's grieving process—and to share in it to the extent that you both find helpful—but you learn not to be threatened by your differences.

If you and your partner are together, know that it will be critical to the health of your relationship for you to communicate with one another. Although you will grieve differently—and most often separately—it is vitally important that you remain connected in some way. Simply sharing highlights of your grief will enable you to have an awareness of your partner's needs, as well as a sense of where they are going on their grief journey.

At times it may be best for you to seek assistance from other people, particularly early on in your grief. In seeking the support of others—and thereby meeting some of your own needs—you will be in a better position to be available to your partner at some level, minimal as that might be for a while.

You may also find that there are periods when you need to give the other person some space in their grief. Part of the grief work that must be done will involve time alone and away from one another. You will each have different styles of grieving and you need room to be able to do what is best for you.

If the child that has died was your only child, you will be left with some difficult questions. If this is your situation you may be asking yourself, "Who am I now that my child has died?" "Am I still a mother?" or "Am I still a father?" When people ask how many children you have, how do you respond? You want to honor the memory of your child, but at the same time it may be too painful to answer this question directly. Some parents have found that there are times when it is easiest to simply state that they have no children, whereas there may be others when they will indicate that they have no living children.

If you and the parent of your child were not in a relationship at the time of your child's death, you have likely lost an important link to one another. Your connection as parents has been severed by the death of your child.

In conclusion, it is important to reiterate that the death of your child has irrevocably changed your life. You have changed and your partner has changed. This means, then, that your relationship with one another must also change. Realizing what this will mean for you both is something that will reveal itself gradually over time as you do the hard work of grief.

RELATIONSHIP WITH YOUR SURVIVING CHILD(REN)

When a child loses a brother or sister, the loss is profound; the implications are far-reaching and lifelong. Having had the firsthand experience of a child's death, their easy sense of innocence—their belief that they are safe and will always be taken care of—has been shattered. Life is encountered with a new sense of vulnerability and a heightened awareness of mortality.

Children may feel a degree of responsibility for their sibling's death, believing that something they said, thought, or did was somehow the cause of it. It will be important for you to clarify with your child the cause of her sibling's death, emphasizing that she is not responsible for it.

In losing a brother or sister, children may also—in a sense—lose their parents. As overwhelmed as you may be in your own grief, for a time this may render you emotionally—possibly even physically—unavailable to your child.

Children's sense of security and well-being stems primarily from their feeling of being taken care of by people they know and trust. When this is threatened or missing, children may feel abandoned, often unable to face what is before them given their limited resources. It will be important for you to ensure for the ongoing care of your children. When possible, ask a person that your child is comfortable with to come to your home for a limited period of time to provide this care. This will allow your child access to you in surroundings that are familiar.

Grief as a child can be an isolating experience. In general, not many of your child's friends or peers will have had a loved one die, particularly not a sibling. Providing your child with the opportunity to interact with other children who have had a brother or sister die is invaluable. Not only does this help your child to feel less isolated in their grief, it also gives them a chance to share their stories and to benefit from one another's experiences.

As a parent having experienced a parent's worst nightmare, the death of a child, you may find that you become overly protective of your remaining children. While it is natural to want to protect your child from that which is harmful, you are painfully aware that this is not always wise or within your power. As scared as you may be, your other children need to be allowed to live a life that offers them the appropriate opportunities for ongoing growth and development.

RELATIONSHIP WITH YOUR PARENTS

When your child dies, your parents face the grief that accompanies the loss of a beloved grandchild. In addition to this, they also experience the agony of seeing you—their child—in excruciating pain, knowing there is little they can do to fix it. Just as you have wanted to make things "all better" for your child, so do your parents. The fact that you are an adult does not change this. As their child, their need to protect and care for you remains.

You may experience your parents as very supportive, finding that you are able to lean on them for guidance and support. If this is the case, it may be helpful to delegate specific tasks to them. Regardless of what they do, by being able to help you in some way, they are—as your parents—indirectly meeting their need to care for you. Although they can't change the fact of your child's death, they can be helpful to you as you face the challenge of rebuilding a life that integrates the memory of your child into it.

If you find your parents so overwhelmed by their own grief that they are unable to be available to you, you may deem it necessary to distance yourself from them on a temporary basis. Immersed as deeply as you are in your own pain, you will have a limited capacity for helping others.

If you seem to be bearing the weight of your parents' grief, consider having someone you trust address this with them. It may be that your parents feel so inadequate or helpless in the face of your pain that they have overlooked the need to seek support for their own. If this is the case, your parents may benefit from a gentle reminder emphasizing the importance of self-care.

Relationship with Your Friends and Colleagues

Friends and colleagues may want to help, but oftentimes they are at a loss as to how to be supportive. In your grieving process, you will gradually learn who are the people who you can count on for support and who are the ones that are unwilling or incapable of providing assistance that is of any benefit to you. Bereaved parents frequently speak of this, often indicating surprise at whom they thought were there friends versus those who actually turned out to be.

As noted previously, at a time when you are most vulnerable, you will likely find that you have the task of educating other people. This may seem highly unfair and frequently overwhelming. The reality is, however, if people have limited experience with death, they may have little or no understanding of the grieving that ensues.

If you do not make the effort—as difficult as this might be—to inform your friends and colleagues about your loss and the implications of it for your life, you may find yourself in the position of having to face any number of expectations that are unintentionally unrealistic.

With a combination of time and hard effort, you will gradually move through the period of acute grief into the longer process of mourning. You will learn how to be present and attentive to your grief and the needs you have regarding it, while also managing to function in your everyday life. You will determine the friends and colleagues that can offer the gift of presence, listening quietly and inviting you to share your story over and over again as a part of your grief journey. When you express a feeling or voice a need, these people won't feel compelled to try to "fix" your grief; they understand the value of allowing you to find your own answers as you search for the meaning of your child's death.

Asking for—and then accepting—the support offered by these particular friends and colleagues is, in a sense, a gift you can give yourself. In the end, if this enables you to let go of the pain of grief—to move to a point where you are able to both celebrate the life and honor the memory of your child—then it will be worth the effort involved.

CHAPTER 6

FINDING SUPPORT FOR YOUR GRIEF

Most parents, states Barbara D. Rosof—through some combination of their own efforts and the passage of more time than they imagined—manage to find their way through grief to a path that leads them toward a life they can live.

In general, bereaved parents emphasize the importance of connecting with other people, indicating the magnitude of the loss is too much to bear alone. Although much of your grief work will be done on your own, the strength and the desire to keep on going come from your connections with other people. The gifts these people can offer—their willingness to listen to you, their respect and understanding of your pain, their unwavering faith in your ability to heal and move forward—these are the things that provide a foundation upon which you can begin the long and difficult process of rebuilding a life without your child.

Many parents say that it was other parents who had also experienced the death of a child who were their greatest help. Although there may be any number of people in your life who genuinely want to help, it is other bereaved parents who can understand your pain in a way that other people cannot.

You can seek the assistance of other bereaved parents through a variety of avenues. These can include: attending a grief support group, participating in a bereavement follow-up or parent-to-parent support program, attending various memorial events, and searching the Internet as a means of seeking information and gaining access to an appropriate chat room.

Although it may be extremely beneficial to connect with other grieving parents—both to gain a perspective on your grief process and to access support and guidance from others who can truly empathize with your loss—there may be situations when this is not enough. Some parents, either temporarily or permanently, become so focused on their loss that they are unable to believe there can be a life beyond it.

Rosof proposes the following factors as barriers to grieving: 1) previous losses, 2) severe stressors, 3) substance abuse, 4) negative responses from family and friends, 5) a highly ambivalent relationship with your child, and 6) personality characteristics that interfere with the establishment of trust.

When considering whether or not you are healing in your grief, timing will be an important factor. If your grief remains intense for a prolonged period of time with no signs of change or improvement, there may be reason for concern. What is important is that there be some movement, however minimal.

If you recognize that you have a problem in your grieving, an essential first step toward resolution has been made. In order for change to actually occur, you need to make the decision that something must be done. No matter what anyone else thinks or says, the motivation for change has to come from within you. Seeking the help of a mental health professional who has knowledge and expertise in the area of grief and bereavement is a good way to take care of yourself.

CHAPTER 7

LIVING WITH GRIEF DURING A LIFETIME

The grieving process has at times been likened to the waves of the ocean. The feelings of grief are natural, often experienced as an ebb and flow of emotion. In this process, we can choose to prepare ourselves to ride with the flow of the water or we can resist the driving force hidden beneath it. In making this choice, it is important to consider that grief is not something that will simply go away with the passage of time or a lack of attention to it. Even if buried deep within our self, the feelings of grief will one day rise again to the surface and command our attention.

The traditional rituals surrounding death (i.e., reviewal, funeral, memorial service) often provide an immediate focus for your attention and offer an element of structure to your day. Once these activities are completed, however, it may feel as if there is little direction to your life. In the initial days, weeks, and likely even months, following the death of your child, your grief may seem all consuming. Getting up each morning and living through each day may be the goal you set for yourself during this time.

As time goes on and the weeks become months, parents often note that there is a shift in the support that is readily available to them. Quickly enough, it seems as if other people move back into the rhythm of their lives, leaving you feeling out of sync and somewhat isolated in your grief. As best you can, surround yourself with those who offer the precious gift of presence, allowing them to listen and respond to your pain while also simultaneously celebrating with you the life of your child.

When thinking of the year immediately following the death of your child, consider the number of "firsts" it will hold (i.e., your child's birthday, Mother's Day, Father's Day, Christmas or Hanukkah, the anniversary of the death). Bereaved parents often talk about how helpful it is to anticipate and plan for these days, stating that the time right before, or immediately after, the particular day is often more difficult than the actual day. Consider what will be helpful to you in remembering and honoring your child and with whom you want to share this. Although there are bound to be those who do not understand or accept your plans, know that it is okay to do what feels most comfortable to you given the rhythm and flow of your grief.

For a long time following the death—likely much longer than you would ever have imagined—you will continue to experience tidal waves of grief. In this process it will be important for you to face all of the feelings that your child's death has evoked in you. At times it may be necessary to fully immerse yourself in these emotions; at one moment feeling tossed about by their forcefulness and in another experiencing the gentle sensation of being slowly rocked by them. In doing this—in letting your emotions completely wash over you—you are allowing some of their power and intensity to be swept away, which allows for healing. Although the grief that you carry remains with you forever, ideally it will become a part of—rather than all of—your life.

As you continue on this journey of grief, know that you have embarked on what will be a lifelong process. The death of your child has affected you deeply and spiritually. What you once thought provided meaning and purpose to your life may now leave you feeling empty. You are faced with the daunting task of redefining for yourself the values and convictions that will help you to move forward without the physical presence of your child. Deep within your soul you will find the answers that enable you to believe that life can again hold promise and meaning and hope.

For many of you, your belief in God (or some other higher power) will sustain you as you grapple with the very mystery of life—that part of it that we cannot understand but somehow struggle courageously to accept. In this process you will define or create some meaning for your child's life and death. You will let go of life as you have known it and move ahead with the memory and spirit of your child carried within your heart.

Right now this may seem overwhelming, perhaps even inconceivable. You have been devastated and it's difficult to imagine life beyond the current moment. You will find, however, that the time will come when your sadness has lightened and memories of your child bring with them a gentle comfort. The waves of emotion, although continuing to wash over you, will do so less often and with decreased intensity. Life will one day hold new hopes and dreams for you, and you will experience again the joy that these can bring forth.

WORKS CITED

Rosof, Barbara D., *The Worst Loss* (New York: Henry Holt and Company, 1994).

Schiff, Harriet Sarnoff, *The Bereaved Parent* (New York: Viking Press, 1978).

Worden, William J., *Grief Counseling and Grief Therapy* (Springer Publishing Company Inc., New York, NY 10012, 1991), used by permission.

CPSIA information can be obtained at www.ICGtesting.com
232481LV00008B/27/P